With Books and Bricks

How Booker T. Washington Built a School

Suzanne Slade

Pictures by
Nicole Tadgell

Albert Whitman & Company
Chicago, Illinois

With love, to my brother Fred—SS

*For Paul, thank you
for believing in me.—NT*

Library of Congress Cataloging-in-Publication data is on file with the publisher.

Text copyright © 2014 by Suzanne Slade
Pictures copyright © 2014 by Nicole Tadgell
Published in 2014 by Albert Whitman & Company
ISBN 978-0-8075-0897-8
Printed in China.
10 9 8 7 6 5 4 3 2 1 BP 18 17 16 15 14

The design is by Nick Tiemersma.

For more information about Albert Whitman & Company,
visit our web site at www.albertwhitman.com.

$\mathcal{F}$ROM SUNRISE TO SUNSET, YOUNG BOOKER WORKED HARD. He carried water to the fields. He carried corn to the mill. He carried rocks from the yard.

All day long, Booker lugged heavy loads with a heavy heart because he was a slave.

But one day he was told to carry something new—books for his master's daughter. When he arrived at the schoolhouse on top of the hill, Booker stole a long look inside.

He saw strange lines on the blackboard that formed letters. He saw groups of letters that made words. And suddenly, Booker's heavy heart felt a little lighter. He knew there was something special about those letters. He felt magic in those words. Booker wanted to learn to read more than anything. But his dream seemed impossible.

After Booker turned nine, America's battle over slavery was finally over. The Civil War had ended. All slaves were free! Booker didn't feel free. He had to work long hours in a salt mine so his family could survive. All the schools near him were for white students only.

So Booker begged his mother for a book of his own. And somehow, as often happens with mothers, a miracle appeared. Without a penny in her pockets, she got Booker an old Webster's spelling book. He studied those shapes called letters. He learned groups of letters that made words. He taught himself to read! But he wanted to learn more.

Then Booker went to work in a coal mine. While shoveling heavy piles of coal all day, he thought of only one thing—school. One morning whispers echoed through the mine.

"A school for black students…"

"Somewhere in Virginia…"

Booker couldn't believe his ears. A school for him!

But Virginia was five hundred miles away. He had no money for a train ticket. No money for books. So Booker kept working and saving and dreaming of school.

In time, he made the long trip to Virginia—walking and begging rides most of the way. At sixteen, Booker finally carried his own books to school.

He graduated three years later and went back to his hometown to teach at a school for black students. He wanted to help others who shared his dream of learning.

Later, folks from a small town in Alabama invited him to teach there. So Booker packed his clothes, books, and watch (the only valuable thing he owned) and moved to the green hills of Tuskegee. He found lots of eager students there—but no school building. Booker searched the town until he found an old shed he could use. The building had no windows or doors and huge holes in the roof, but it was all he had.

Soon, the whole town of Tuskegee was talking about Booker's school. Dozens of students lined up the first day. They squished and squeezed inside the tiny shed. Each week the school became more crowded. When it rained, students took turns holding an umbrella over Booker so he could keep teaching.

Booker knew his students needed a real building. A school of their own. So he decided to build one—brick by brick.

Booker borrowed money to buy a deserted farm. He cleared twenty acres of land.

Then came the hard part—getting bricks to build the school walls. With no brickyard in town, Booker decided to make his own. He read about different kinds of clay. He studied how to mold and bake bricks. He learned how to lay them into tall, sturdy walls.

Soon, Booker and his students
started digging for clay. They dug
for hours. They dug for days.
   But no clay.

They dug bigger holes.
They dug huge muddy pits.

Still no clay!

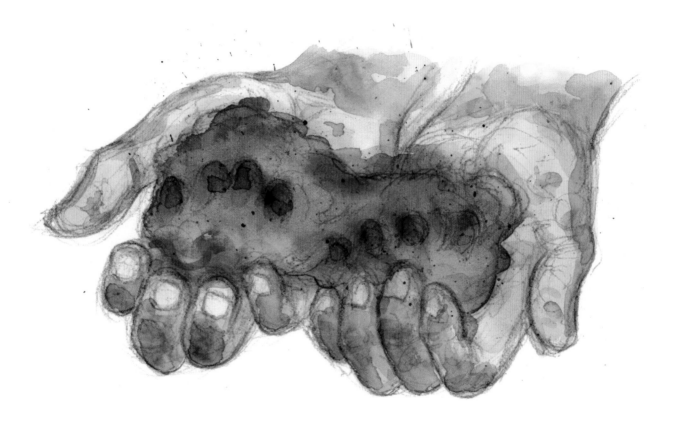

Booker's hands blistered. His tired back ached. He was covered in mud and his knees were caked. But he kept digging until he found it—rich, red Alabama clay.

Booker and his students mixed mud into the clay, then added straw to hold the sticky mixture together. They molded the mixture into thick slabs and smoothed the sides straight. They molded and smoothed again and again.

They made twenty-five thousand bricks.

Then Booker built a mighty kiln. He filled it with thousands of clay slabs and fanned the flames till they burned red hot. The wet bricks started to sizzle, and then the kiln broke. All the bricks were ruined!

Students made thousands more bricks. Booker built a second kiln but it broke too. The students were exhausted. They wanted to quit. But Booker wouldn't give up. Other teachers joined the tired work crew. They helped build a third kiln. It failed after burning a week—more useless bricks!

With no money to build another kiln, the teachers told Booker to forget about making bricks. To stop wasting his time. Time.

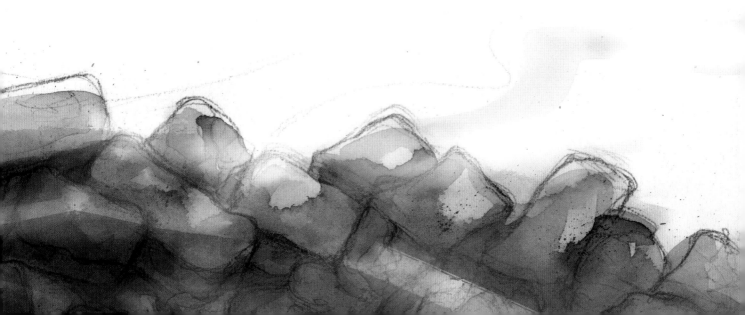

Then Booker remembered his precious watch.
He decided to sell it to pay for another kiln. This
oven baked just right and made beautiful bricks.
Booker was finally ready to build a school!

Students mixed up big buckets of mortar. Booker grabbed a trowel and spread the mortar, smooth and even. He gently tapped brick after brick into place.

Four sturdy walls rose from the ground. Windows were hung. Hammers started to pound.

Students nailed on a new waterproof
roof. Then Booker installed a fine front
door—a door to welcome everyone.

More students kept arriving, so Booker kept building.
More digging. More molding. More bricks were baked.
More fingers blistered. More tired backs ached.

New buildings appeared—a dining hall, a chapel, and a dorm where students could live.

Students built chairs, tables, and beds from wood scraps. They filled cloth sacks with pine needles to make mattresses. Now Booker's school was big enough for everyone who wanted to learn. His hardworking students went on to become successful teachers, business leaders, and more.

Because Booker T. Washington had built
an amazing school—brick by brick!

"Success is to be measured not so much by the position that one has reached in life, as by the obstacles which he has overcome while trying to succeed."

—Booker T. Washington

More about Booker

As a boy, Booker T. Washington thought school "must be the greatest place on earth."

When slavery ended in 1865, Booker's town didn't have any schools for black students. Months later, a man moved into town and started a makeshift school for blacks. After pleading with his stepfather, Booker was briefly allowed to meet with the teacher. But before long, his stepfather ended his schooling, and said Booker had to work more hours to help support the family. Then Booker heard about Hampton Normal and Industrial Institute for black students, where he could attend classes while working to pay for school. So Booker begged rides from strangers and walked many hilly miles to make the five-hundred-mile trip to Hampton Normal. He arrived with only a small satchel of clothes and fifty cents. Booker found a janitor job to pay for his room and food, and the principal arranged for a donor to pay his tuition.

After graduating with honors in 1875, Booker became a teacher. First, he taught at a school for black students in his hometown of Malden, West Virginia, then went back to Hampton Institute and taught there for two years. In 1881, he moved to Tuskegee, Alabama, to start a brand-new school. When it opened on July 4, 1881, thirty students (half young men and half young women) signed up immediately. Some of his students were adult teachers who wanted to learn more. At first, Booker used a dilapidated shack for a classroom. By the end of the month, the tiny shack was packed with fifty students. A teacher named Miss Davidson soon arrived to help the growing school. Then Booker looked for land to build a new school. He found a rundown plantation nearby and borrowed money from an old friend for a down payment and agreed to pay the rest later. The one thousand acre plantation had four buildings—a cabin, kitchen, stable, and henhouse—which Booker used for classes while he drew up plans for a school made of sturdy bricks. Miss Davidson held festivals and other events to raise money for building supplies.

Booker's students became frustrated with the backbreaking task of making and laying bricks, but his passion for learning and teaching inspired them to continue the exhausting work. Although he taught "book learning" such as multiplication, geography, and grammar, Booker believed it was important for his students to learn new trade skills that could help them earn a living. As Booker explained, "My plan was not to teach them to work in the old way, but to show them how to make the forces of nature—air, water, steam, electricity, horse-power—assist them in their labour."

Booker later became a famous speaker and traveled around the country sharing his ideas about education. But he never forgot about the school he built—Tuskegee Normal and Industrial Institute.

He continued to help improve and expand it until his death in 1915. At that time Tuskegee Institute had one hundred buildings and fifteen hundred students. Through the years, thousands of lives have been changed because of Booker's hard work and determination, and the fine school he built—brick by brick.

Bibliography

"History of Tuskegee University." Tuskegee University. 2014. http://www.tuskegee.edu/about_us/history_and_mission.aspx.

Washington, Booker T. *An Autobiography: The Story of My Life and Work*. Atlanta: J. L. Nichols, 1901. Accessed through Google Books. http://ittybittyurl.com/Wx0.

Washington, Booker T. *Up from Slavery*. New York: Dodd, Mead & Company, 1965.

Source Notes for Quotes

p. 8: "One day, while at work in the coal-mine, I happened to overhear two miners talking about a great school for coloured people somewhere in Virginia." Washington, *Up from Slavery*, p. 27.

p. 29: "Success is to be…while trying to succeed." Washington, *Up from Slavery*, p. 25.

p. 30: "As they went on describing the school, it seemed to me that it must be the greatest place on earth." Washington, *Up from Slavery*, p. 27.

p. 31: "My plan was…them in their labour." Washington, *Up from Slavery*, p. 94.

Author's Note

The idea for this book began years ago when I was writing another children's book, *Booker T. Washington: Teacher, Speaker, Leader*. During my research I read Washington's autobiography, *Up from Slavery*, and heard in his own words the story I'd read in many children's books—how he'd pursued his education after slavery ended. But I also discovered details about a part of his life I'd heard little about—how he painstakingly built a school so others could fulfill their dreams of an education too.

Booker faced many challenges while building Tuskegee Normal and Industrial Institute, but he encountered even more as he led the school over the next thirty-four years. When the school's bills came due each month, Booker spent many sleepless nights figuring out how he would pay them. When the cold winter winds howled, Booker searched for coats to keep his students warm. And when his tired students had no place to sleep, Booker filled cloth bags with pine needles to make mattresses. Through it all, Booker persevered because he cared deeply for his students and believed they deserved a school of their own.